DUETS in Color
Book 2

12 Original Duets in Minor Keys

by Naoko Ikeda

ISBN 978-1-61780-865-4

EXCLUSIVELY DISTRIBUTED BY

WILLIS MUSIC

HAL•LEONARD®
CORPORATION
7777 W. BLUEMOUND RD. P.O. BOX 13819
MILWAUKEE, WISCONSIN 53213

Visit Hal Leonard Online at
www.halleonard.com

Foreword

I love piano duets, and it has been my dream to write duets in all 24 keys for a long time. I am happy to finally be able to present them to you in these two volumes called *Duets in Color*. Although they are presented separately in major and minor keys, I highly recommend performing them in pairs, e.g. "Scarlet Hearts" (D Major) in *Book 1*, and "Misty Rose" (D Minor) in *Book 2*.

We are fortunate to live in a beautiful world that is rich in amazing colors. My sincere hope is that these pieces help you to see them more clearly.

Naoko Ikeda

Biography

Naoko Ikeda lives in Sapporo, Hokkaido in northern Japan. Influenced by classical music, jazz and pop, as well as the piano works of William Gillock, her own music reflects her diverse tastes with beauty, elegance, and humor. Ms. Ikeda holds a piano performance degree from Yamaguchi College of Arts (Japan) and currently maintains an energetic schedule as both teacher and composer.

Contents

Silver Rain

Naoko Ikeda

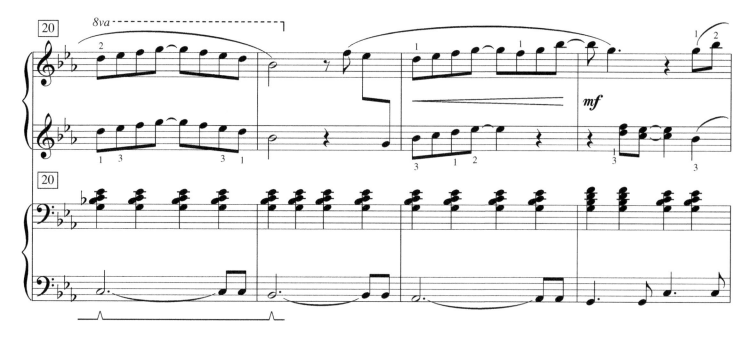

Orange Flames at Night*

for Hitomi Ogawa

Naoko Ikeda

* Previously published as "Hot Night."

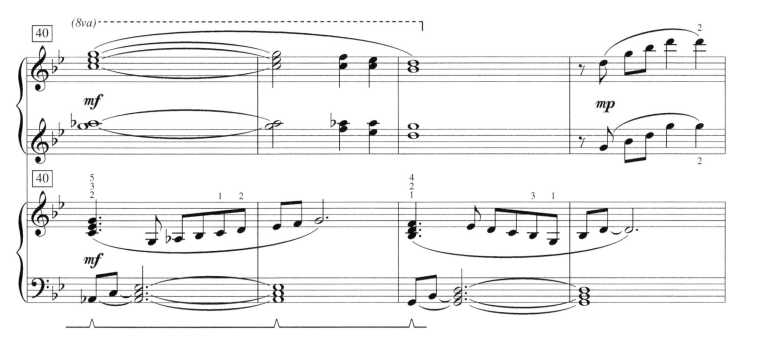

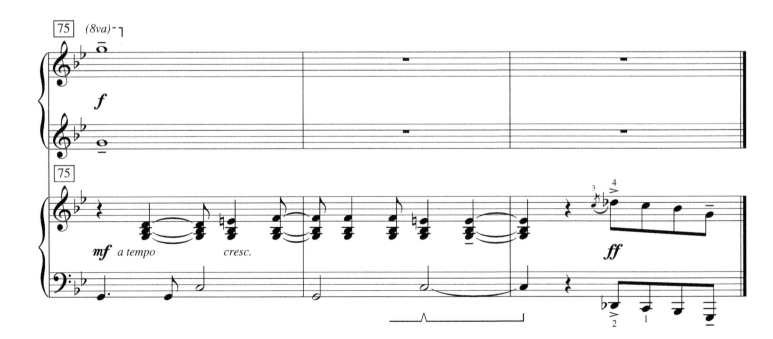

Misty Rose

for Kaya Matsubara & Naomi Fukui

Naoko Ikeda

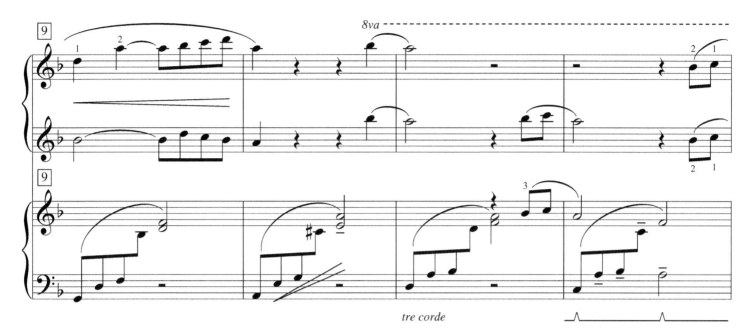

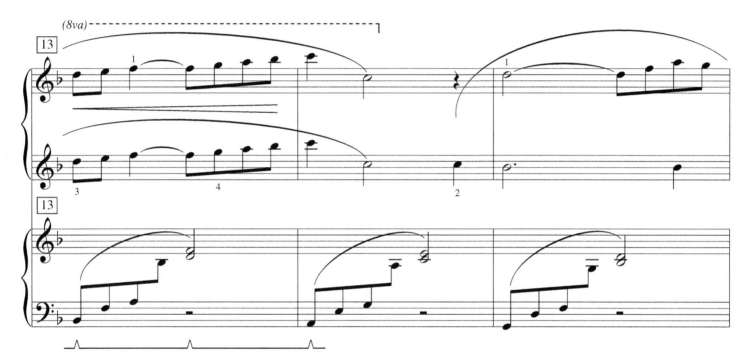

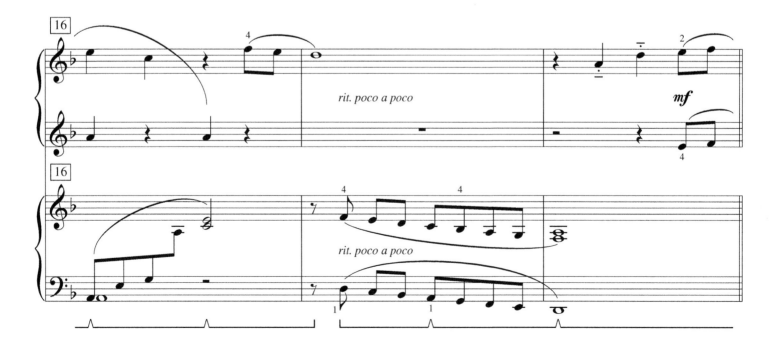

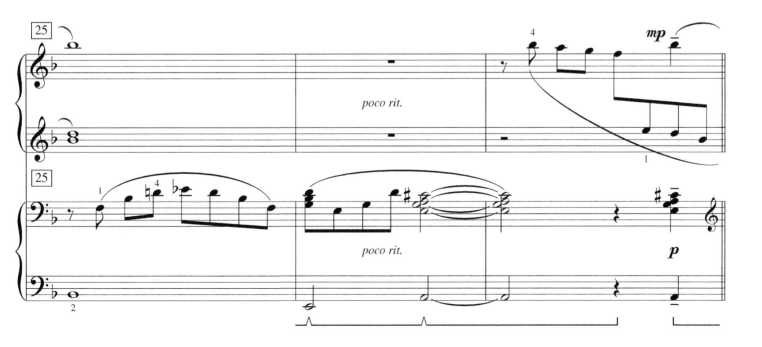

una corda

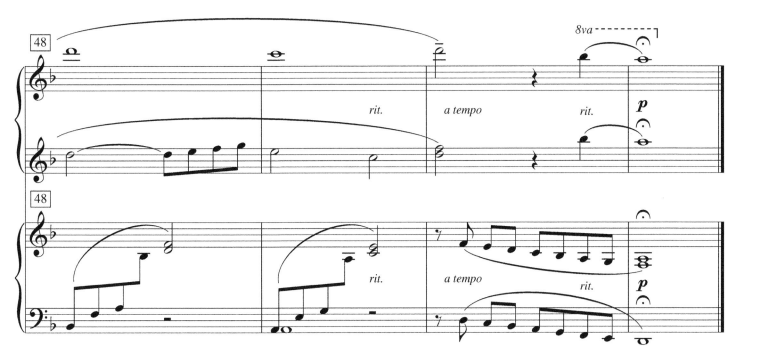

Azure Jewels
(Lapis Lazuli)

for Chikako Kunisue, Reiko Tamura, Kozui Kitakamae & Kyoko Sawano

Naoko Ikeda

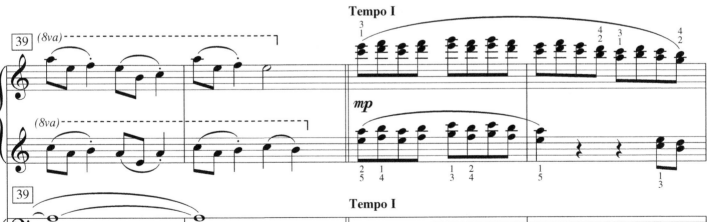

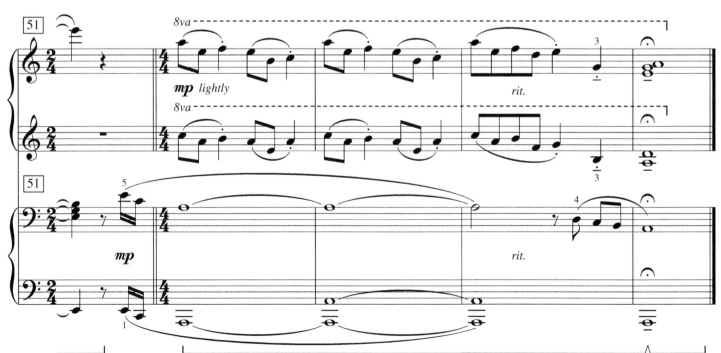

Sapphire Blossoms

for Yoko Maeda & Atsuko Okano

Naoko Ikeda

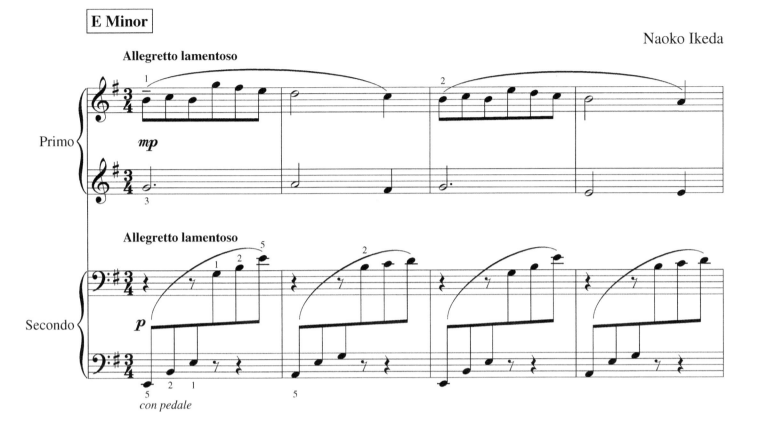

Gray Skies

for Yūka & Sazuki Murakami

Naoko Ikeda

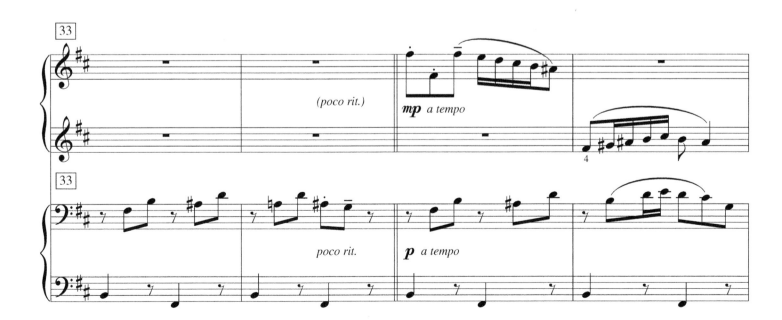

Midnight Blue Ballade

Naoko Ikeda

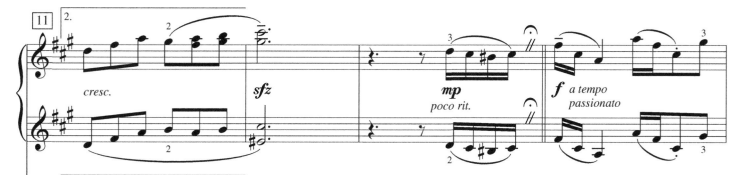

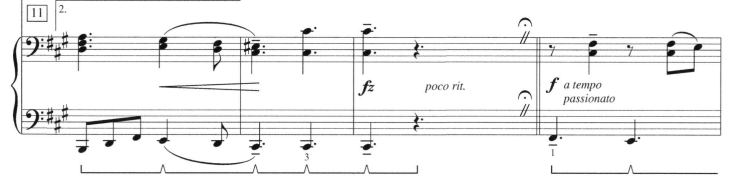

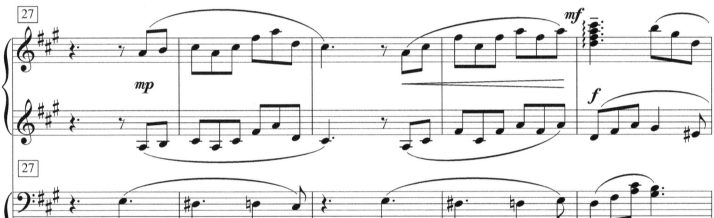

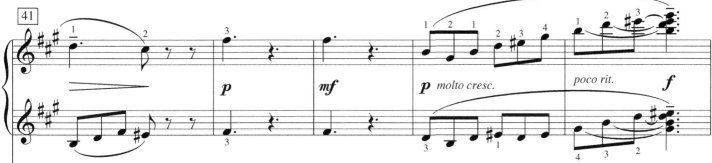

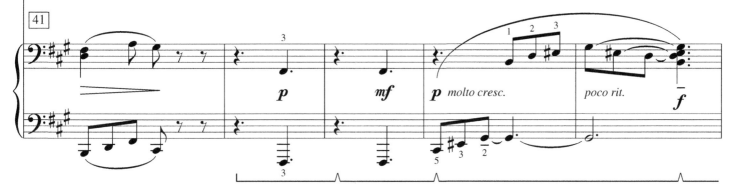

Cool Chartreuse

for Kevin Cranley

Naoko Ikeda

Rondo in Red

Naoko Ikeda

NOTE: The right hand of the Secondo plays over (on top of) the left hand of the Primo in measures 1–4.

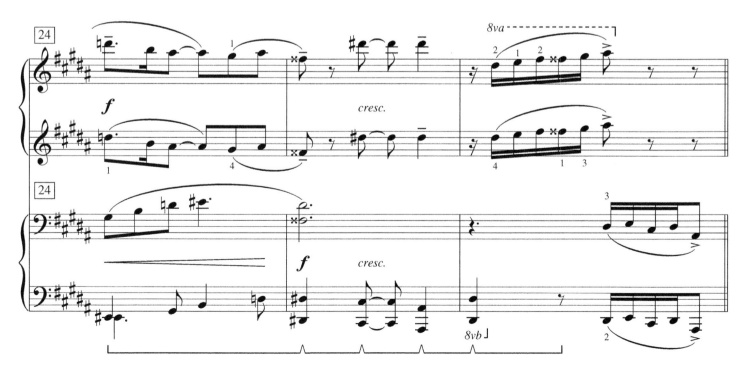

Sepia Memories

for Shigehisa Tanaka

Naoko Ikeda

E♭ Minor

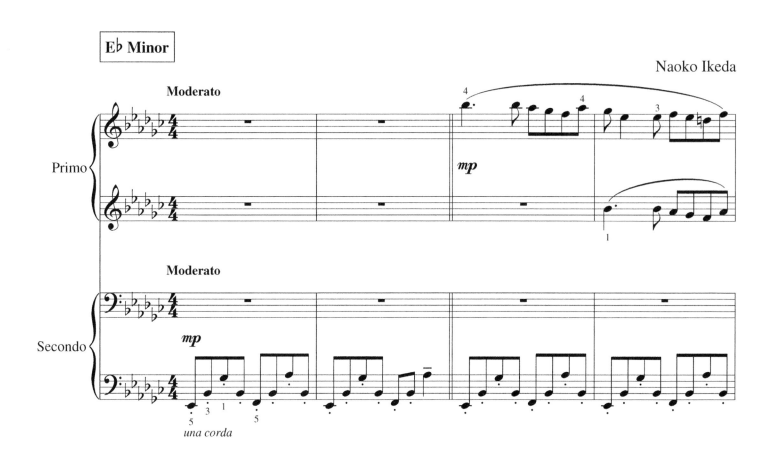

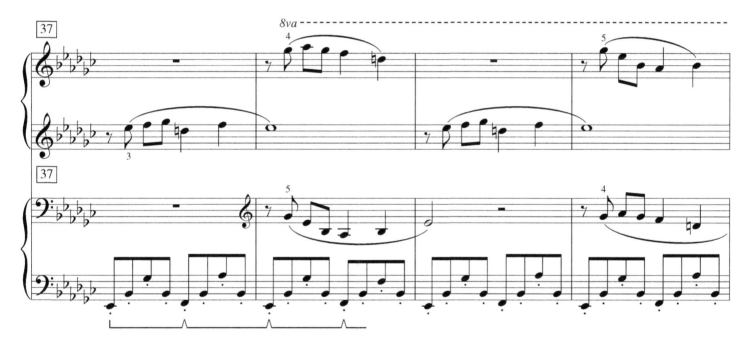

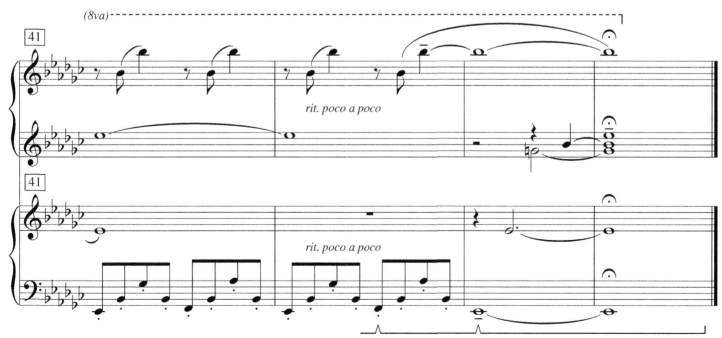

Snow Fantasy

for Azusa Uda

Naoko Ikeda

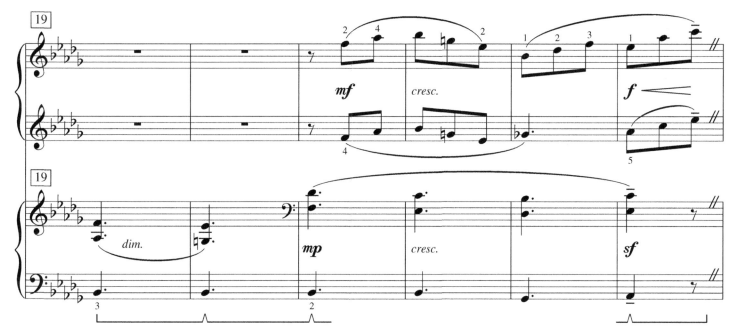

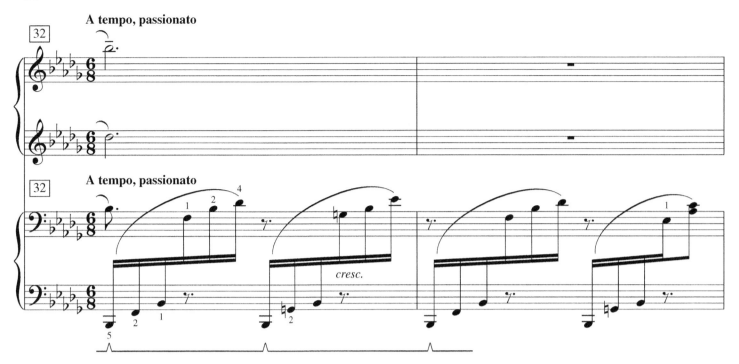

Burgundy Shadows*

for Harumi Inoue

Naoko Ikeda

* Previously published as "Shadow of Wine."

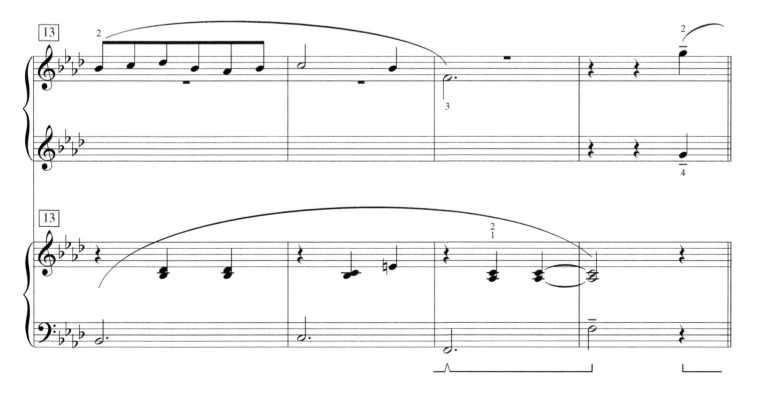

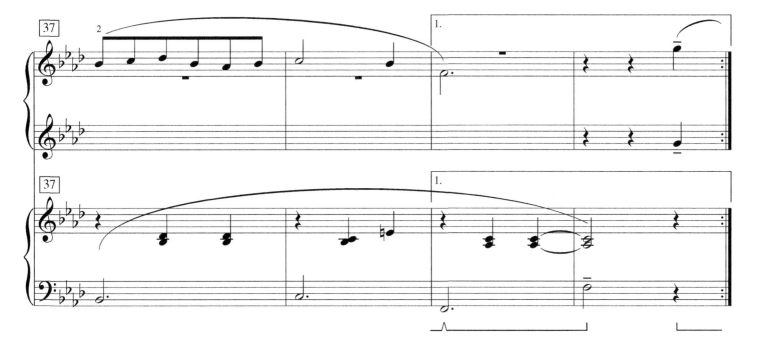

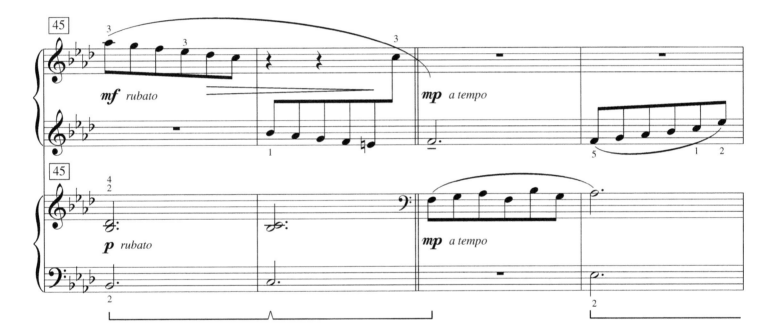

Dynamic Duets
and Exciting Ensembles from Willis Music!

SELECTED COLLECTIONS

00416804	Accent on Duets (MI-LI) / *William Gillock*	$12.99
00416822	All-American Ragtime Duets (EI) / *Glenda Austin*	$7.99
00416732	Concerto No. 1 for Piano and Strings (MI) (2P, 4H) / *Alexander Peskanov*	$14.95
00416898	Duets in Color Book 1 (EI-MI) / *Naoko Ikeda*	$12.99

00138687	5 Easy Duets (EE-ME) / *Carolyn Miller*	$7.99
00406230	First Piano Duets (EE) / *John Thompson* series	$4.95
00416805	New Orleans Jazz Styles Duets (EI) / *Gillock, arr. Austin*	$9.99
00416830	Teaching Little Fingers Easy Duets (EE) / *arr. Miller*	$6.99

SELECTED SHEETS

Early Elementary

00125695	The Knights' Quest (1P, 4H) / *Wendy Stevens*	$3.99
00406743	Wisteria (1P, 4H) / *Carolyn C. Setliff*	$2.95

Mid-Elementary

00412289	Andante Theme from "Surprise Symphony" (1P, 8H) / *Haydn, arr. Bilbro*	$2.95
00406208	First Jazz (1P, 4H) / *Melody Bober*	$2.50

Later Elementary

00415178	Changing Places (1P, 4H) / *Edna Mae Burnam*	$3.99
00406209	Puppy Pranks (1P, 4H) / *Melody Bober*	$2.50
00416864	Rockin' Ragtime Boogie (1P, 4H) / *Glenda Austin*	$3.99
00120780	Strollin' (1P, 4H) / *Carolyn Miller*	$3.99

Early Intermediate

00113157	Dance in the City (1P, 4H) / *Naoko Ikeda*	$3.99
00416843	Festive Celebration (1P, 4H) / *Carolyn Miller*	$3.99
00114960	Fountain in the Rain (1P, 4H) / *William Gillock, arr. Austin*	$3.99
00416854	A Little Bit of Bach (1P, 4H) / *Glenda Austin*	$3.99
00158602	Reflections of You (1P, 4H) / *Randall Hartsell*	$3.99
00416921	Tango in D Minor (IP, 4H) / *Carolyn Miller*	$3.99
00416955	Tango Nuevo (1P, 4H) / *Eric Baumgartner*	$3.99

Mid-Intermediate

00411831	Ave Maria (2P, 4H) / *Bach-Gounod, arr. Hinman*	$2.95
00410726	Carmen Overture (1P, 6H) / *Bizet, arr. Sartorio*	$3.95
00404388	Champagne Toccata (2P, 8H) / *William Gillock*	$3.99
00405212	Dance of the Sugar Plum Fairy / *Tchaikovsky, arr. Gillock*	$3.99
00416959	Samba Sensation (1P, 4H) / *Glenda Austin*	$3.99
00405657	Valse Elegante (1P, 4H) / *Glenda Austin*	$3.99
00149102	Weekend in Paris (1P, 4H) / *Naoko Ikeda*	$3.99

Later Intermediate

00415223	Concerto Americana (2P, 4H) / *John Thompson*	$5.99
00405552	España Cañi (1P, 4H) / *Marquina, arr. Gillock*	$3.99
00405409	March of the Three Kings (1P, 4H) / *Bizet, arr. Gillock*	$2.95

Advanced

00411832	Air (2P, 4H) / *Bach, arr. Hinman*	$2.95
00405663	Habañera (1P, 4H) / *Stephen Griebling*	$2.95
00405299	Jesu, Joy of Man's Desiring (1P, 4H) / *Bach, arr. Gillock*	$3.99
00405648	Pavane (1P, 4H) / *Fauré, arr. Carroll*	$2.95

CLOSER LOOK

View sample pages and hear audio excerpts online at **www.halleonard.com**.

www.willispianomusic.com

Prices, contents, and availability subject to change without notice.

Spectacular Piano Solos

from

www.willispianomusic.com

Early Elementary

00416850	Barnyard Strut/*Glenda Austin*	$2.99
00416702	Big Green Frog/*Carolyn C. Setliff*	$2.99
00416904	The Blizzard/*Glenda Austin*	$2.99
00416882	Bow-Wow Blues/*Glenda Austin*	$2.99
00406670	Cookies/*Carolyn Miller*	$2.99
00404218	Fog at Sea/*William Gillock*	$2.99
00416907	Guardian Angels/*Naoko Ikeda*	$3.99
00416918	Halloween Surprise/*Ronald Bennett*	$2.99
00412099	Moccasin Dance/*John Thompson*	$2.99
00416783	My Missing Teeth/*Carolyn C. Setliff*	$2.95
00416933	The Perceptive Detective/*Carolyn Miller*	$2.99
00416816	Rain, Rain/*Carolyn Miller*	$2.99

Mid-Elementary

00416780	The Acrobat/*Carolyn Miller*	$2.99
00416041	Autumn Is Here/*William Gillock*	$3.99
00416803	The Dancing Bears/*Carolyn Miller*	$2.99
00416878	Mini Toccata/*Eric Baumgartner*	$2.99
00416958	Miss Kitty Kat/*Glenda Austin*	$2.99
00404738	Moonlight/*William Gillock*	$3.99
00416872	The Rainbow/*Carolyn Miller*	$2.99
00416728	Seahorse Serenade/*Carolyn C. Setliff*	$2.95
00416674	Seaside Dancer/*Ronald Bennett*	$2.50

Later Elementary

00416852	Black Cat Chat/*Eric Baumgartner*	$2.99
00416786	Egyptian Journey/*Randall Hartsell*	$2.95
00416906	Evening Melody/*Naoko Ikeda*	$3.99
00416886	Flying Fingers/*Carolyn C. Setliff*	$3.99
00416836	The Gentle Brook/*Carolyn Miller*	$2.99
00416908	The Goblins Gather/*Frank Levin*	$2.99
00405918	Monkey on a Stick/*Lynn Freeman Olson*	$2.95
00416866	October Leaves/*Carolyn C. Setliff*	$2.99
00406552	Parisian Waltz/*Robert Donahue*	$2.95
00416781	The Race Car/*Carolyn Miller*	$2.99
00406564	Showdown/*Ronald Bennett*	$2.99
00416919	Sparkling Waterfall/*Carolyn C. Setliff*	$2.99
00416820	Star Wonders/*Randall Hartsell*	$2.99
00416779	Sunrise at San Miguel/*Ronald Bennett*	$3.99
00416881	Twilight Tarantella/*Glenda Austin*	$2.99

Early Intermediate

00416943	Autumn Nocturne/*Susan Alcon*	$2.99
00405455	Bass Train Boogie/*Stephen Adoff*	$2.99
00416817	Broken Arm Blues/*Carolyn Miller*	$2.99
00416841	The Bubbling Brook/*Carolyn Miller*	$2.99
00416849	Bye-Bye Blues/*Glenda Austin*	$2.99
00416945	Cafe Francais/*Jonathan Maiocco*	$2.99
00416834	Canopy of Stars/*Randall Hartsell*	$2.99
00416956	Dancing in a Dream/*William Gillock*	$3.99
00415585	Flamenco/*William Gillock*	$2.99
00416856	Garden of Dreams/*Naoko Ikeda*	$2.99
00416818	Majestic Splendor/*Carolyn C. Setliff*	$2.99
00416948	Manhattan Swing/*Naoko Ikeda*	$2.99
00416733	The Matador/*Carolyn Miller*	$3.99

00416940	Medieval Rondo/*Carolyn C. Setliff*	$2.99
00416942	A Melancholy Night/*Naoko Ikeda*	$3.99
00416877	Mystic Quest/*Randall Hartsell*	$2.99
00416873	Le Papillon (The Butterfly)/*Glenda Austin*	$2.99
00416829	Scherzo Nuovo/*Eric Baumgartner*	$2.99
00416947	Snowflakes in Spring/*Naoko Ikeda*	$2.99
00416937	Stampede/*Carolyn Miller*	$2.99
00416917	Supernova/*Ronald Bennett*	$2.99
00416842	Tarantella in G Minor/*Glenda Austin*	$3.99
00416782	Toccata Caprice/*Carolyn C. Setliff*	$2.95
00416938	Toccatina Tag/*Ronald Bennett*	$2.99
00416869	Twilight Tapestry/*Randall Hartsell*	$2.99
00416924	A Waltz to Remember/*Glenda Austin*	$3.99

Mid-Intermediate

00416911	Blues Streak/*Eric Baumgartner*	$2.99
00416855	Dance of the Unicorn/*Naoko Ikeda*	$2.99
00416893	Fantasia in A Minor/*Randall Hartsell*	$2.99
00416821	Foggy Blues/*Naoko Ikeda*	$3.99
00414908	Fountain in the Rain/*William Gillock*	$3.99
00416765	Grand Sonatina in G/*Glenda Austin*	$2.95
00416875	Himalayan Grandeur/*Randall Hartsell*	$2.99
00406630	Jazz Suite No. 2/*Glenda Austin*	$4.99
00416910	Little Rock (& Roll)/*Eric Baumgartner*	$3.99
00416939	Midnight Fantasy/*Carolyn C. Setliff*	$2.99
00416857	Moonlight Rose/*Naoko Ikeda*	$2.99
00414627	Portrait of Paris/*William Gillock*	$2.99
00405171	Sea Nocturne/*Glenda Austin*	$2.99
00416844	Sea Tempest/*Randall Hartsell*	$2.99
00415517	Sonatine/*William Gillock*	$4.99
00416701	Spanish Romance/*arr. Frank Levin*	$2.95
00416946	Stormy Seas/*Carolyn Miller*	$3.99
00416100	Three Jazz Preludes/*William Gillock*	$4.99

Later Intermediate

00416764	Romantic Rhapsody/*Glenda Austin*	$4.99
00405646	Soft Lights/*Carolyn Jones Campbell*	$2.99
00409464	Tarantella/*A. Pieczonka*	$3.99

Early Advanced

00415263	Impromptu/*Mildred T. Souers*	$2.99
00415166	Sleighbells in the Snow/*William Gillock*	$4.99
00405264	Valse Brillante/*Glenda Austin*	$4.99

HAL•LEONARD® CORPORATION

7777 W. BLUEMOUND RD. P.O. BOX 13819 MILWAUKEE, WI 53213

CLOSER LOOK — View sample pages and hear audio excerpts online at **www.halleonard.com**

 www.facebook.com/willispianomusic

Prices & availability subject to change without notice.

0322